Sulfur

Richard Beatty

BENCHMARK BOOKS

MARSHALL CAVENDISH

NEW YORK

Benchmark Books
Marshall Cavendish Corporation
99 White Plains Road
Tarrytown, New York 10591

Library of Congress Cataloging-in-Publication Data
Beatty, Richard.
Sulfur / Richard Beatty.
p.   cm. — (The elements)
Includes index.
Summary: Explores the history of the bright-colored nonmetal
sulfur and explains its chemistry, how it reacts, its uses, and
its importance in our lives.
ISBN 0-7614-0948-3 (lib. bdg.)
1. Sulfur—Juvenile literature. [1. Sulfur.] I. Title.
II. Series: Elements (Benchmark Books)
QD181.A4 F37 2001
546'.673—dc21   99-049671 CIP AC

Printed in Hong Kong

Picture credits
Front cover: Mike McNamee/Science Photo Library.
Back cover: Nathan Benn/Corbis (UK) Ltd.
AKG London: Erich Lessing 8.
Corbis (UK) Ltd.: Annie Griffiths Belt 30; Corbis (UK) Ltd. 4; George Lepp 21; Gianni Dagli Orti 25;
José Manuel Sanchis Calvete 10; J. Sohm/ChromoSohm 19; Jonathan Blair 23;
Lester V. Bergman 6; Michael S. Yamashita 9; Nathan Benn 11.
Image Select: Ann Ronan 18.
Leslie Garland Picture Library: Andrew Lambert 12, 17.
Science Photo Library: Charles D. Winters 15; Mike McNamee *i*, 7;
National Institutes of Health *iii*, 27; Professor J. Watson/University of Southampton 26.
Tony Stone Images: Daniel J. Cox 22; David Job 14; David Woodfall 16.

Series created by Brown Partworks Ltd.
Designed by wda

Contents

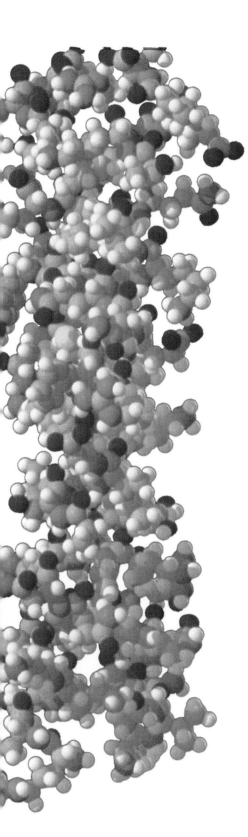

What is sulfur?

Sulfur is a bright yellow nonmetal. It is vital to the inorganic chemical industry and has been used in medicine for a long time. Sulfur is common on Earth, sometimes in the native, or uncombined, form but more often combined with other elements as compounds. Sulfur is also present in meteorites, on other planets, and in the space between stars.

Pure sulfur has no taste or odor and is not harmful to people. However, many of its compounds smell very strongly and some are extremely poisonous.

The sulfur atom

Atoms are the building blocks of all the elements. At the center of each atom is a nucleus, which contains tiny positively

---

SULFUR FACTS

○ **Chemical symbol** S

○ **Atomic number** 16

○ **Relative atomic mass** 32.06. The relative atomic mass measures the average amount of matter in the atom and is effectively equal to the number of protons and neutrons, since electrons are so light.

○ **Melting point** Alpha sulfur: 235°F (112.8°C). Beta sulfur: 246°F (118.9°C)

○ **Boiling point** 832°F (444.7°C)

○ **Specific gravity** Alpha sulfur: 2.07. In other words, alpha sulfur weighs 2.07 times more than the same volume of water.

Volcanic activity on the innermost of Jupiter's four moons, Io, is a strong indication that sulfur is present in large quantities. Astronomers think that the black, red, and orange features on the surface of the moon are volcanic flows of liquid sulfur.

charged particles called protons. Sulfur has an atomic number of 16, which means that the nucleus contains 16 protons. The nucleus also contains neutrons, which have no electrical charge. Most sulfur atoms contain 16 neutrons in the nucleus.

Even smaller negatively charged particles called electrons spin around the nucleus. The number of electrons is always the same as the number of protons, so

every atom of sulfur has 16 electrons orbiting the nucleus. Electrons in atoms are arranged in electron shells. Sulfur has three shells. The first two shells are filled up and contain two and eight electrons respectively. The third shell is only partially filled and contains six electrons.

Atoms are stable if their outer electron shell is full. Atoms will try to gain, lose, or share electrons with other atoms so that all the atoms involved end up with filled shells. As electrons are transferred in a reaction, they form bonds between the atoms, resulting in molecules and compounds.

SULFUR ATOM

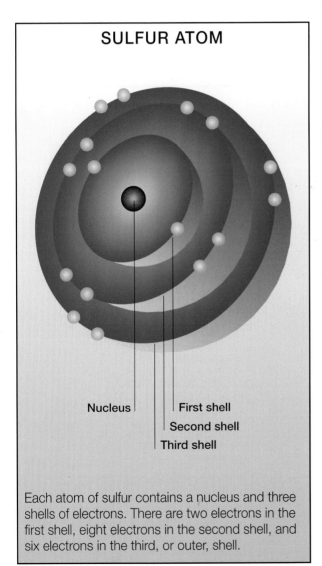

Nucleus | First shell
Second shell
Third shell

Each atom of sulfur contains a nucleus and three shells of electrons. There are two electrons in the first shell, eight electrons in the second shell, and six electrons in the third, or outer, shell.

Forms of sulfur

Sulfur exists in several different solid forms, called allotropes, each with different physical properties. The two most important allotropes are alpha sulfur and beta sulfur. Each allotrope consists of eight sulfur atoms bonded together as a ring-shaped molecule. Alpha sulfur and beta sulfur differ, however, in how the sulfur molecules pack together to form crystals.

Alpha sulfur forms amber crystals in an arrangement called the orthorhombic system. This form is stable below 205°F (96°C). Beta-sulfur forms bright yellow chisel-like crystals in an arrangement called the monoclinic system, which is stable from 205°F (96°C) to the melting point, 246°F (118.9°C). A third form, called plastic sulfur, can be made pouring molten sulfur into cold water. Plastic sulfur is soft

This picture shows amber crystals of alpha sulfur. With alpha sulfur, ring-shaped molecules of sulfur pack together as an orthorhombic crystal system.

This picture shows a polarized light micrograph of crystals of pure sulfur. All crystals form in one of seven categories, called the crystal systems. Sulfur can form crystals in more than one crystal system.

and rubbery and is made of long chains of sulfur atoms. Other forms, such as roll sulfur and flowers of sulfur, contain a mixture of different sulfur allotropes.

Heating sulfur

Molten sulfur also has different physical characteristics, depending on how hot the sulfur is. Just above its melting point, sulfur is a runny amber liquid. If more heat is applied, the molten sulfur thickens and darkens, because the ring-shaped molecules break apart and form long jumbled chains. Near the boiling point of

sulfur, the long chains begin to fall apart, and the sulfur turns into a black liquid.

Using the element

The main use of sulfur is to make sulfuric acid, but it is also used as a fungicide (a chemical that destroys fungi) and in medicine to treat certain skin conditions. Recently, people have found uses for sulfur in construction. For example, sulfur-based concretes, cements, and wall coatings are used where resistance to chemical attack is important. Large amounts of sulfur are used in the vulcanization of rubber.

Early history

People have known about sulfur since prehistoric times, when the element was used as a pigment for cave paintings. However, the first people to find practical and industrial uses for sulfur were probably the ancient Egyptians. They used it in medicine and burned it to create fumes for bleaching cotton cloth. Sulfur fumes were also used to kill household pests. Greek scholar Homer mentions this use in his epic poem the *Odyssey,* which dates back to the eighth century B.C.E.

Sulfur was first used in explosives and fire displays around 1,000 years ago in China. As trade routes opened between Europe and the Far East, sulfur became increasingly important as a constituent (part) of gunpowder. The advent of the industrial revolution in the 18th century led to a dramatic increase in the use of sulfur, especially in the manufacture of sulfuric acid. Today, more sulfur is used worldwide than ever before.

Chemical understanding

Sulfur was recognized as an important substance long before the science of chemistry began to develop. Arab alchemists (medieval scientists who studied chemistry and medicine), for example, believed that all substances were made of two basic "principles," sulfur and mercury. However, the modern idea of chemical elements developed in the 18th century from the work of French chemist Antoine Lavoisier (1743–1794). Along with sulfur, Lavoisier listed over 30 other substances that he believed to be chemical elements.

French artist Jacques Louis David (1748–1825) completed this painting of French chemist Antoine Lavoisier and his wife in 1788.

Obtaining sulfur

Steam rises from a sulfur-encrusted vent on Mount Tozan on the Japanese island of Hokkaido.

Although it is one of the less common elements in Earth's crust, sulfur is widely distributed across our planet as pure deposits and in combination with other elements as rocks and minerals. Many scientists believe that deeper layers of the earth contain much larger deposits of the element. Beneath the surface, most sulfur is combined in sulfide minerals such as pyrite (iron sulfide, or FeS_2). Sulfur may also exist in the form of hydrogen sulfide gas (H_2S). This gas is released during volcanic activity, and it is transformed into elemental sulfur by reacting with oxygen in the air as it reaches Earth's surface.

Huge deposits of the compound calcium sulfate ($CaSO_4$) also exist underground. These deposits were formed by the evaporation of seas and lagoons millions of years ago. Over time, the deposits became buried. Some underground salt deposits, called salt domes, contain pure sulfur. Sulfur compounds are also found in fossil fuels such as coal and oil.

SULFUR SOURCES FACTS

Source	Notes
Native sulfur (S)	Underground deposits of very pure sulfur are extracted using a process developed by Herman Frasch.
Iron sulfide (FeS$_2$) Occurs as the mineral iron pyrite, more commonly called pyrite.	Iron pyrite was the main source of sulfur before the development of the Frasch process. Iron pyrite is still the main source in countries such as China.
Calcium sulfate (CaSO$_4$) Occurs in the minerals gypsum and anhydrite.	These minerals were often converted to sulfur in the past. However, the process is not currently practical since too much energy input is needed.
Hydrogen sulfide (H$_2$S) Recovered from fossil fuels.	Sulfur recovered from fossil fuels is now the biggest single source of the element in the United States.
Sulfur dioxide (SO$_2$) A by-product of smelting reactions.	Sulfur dioxide is the starting chemical in the contact process—the industrial preparation of sulfuric acid.

Nearer Earth's surface, where oxygen is more plentiful, sulfate minerals (containing sulfur and oxygen) are more common. Seawater also contains large quantities of sulfur in the form of sulfate ions.

Obtaining pure sulfur

Up until the early 19th century, the main source of sulfur in Europe was the deposits on the island of Sicily. Extracting the sulfur was a crude process. The sulfur-bearing rock was piled into mounds and heated at the top, which melted elemental sulfur in the rock layers below. The molten sulfur poured out from the bottom of the pile and was collected for further refining. In other parts of the world, such as Japan,

Pyrite (iron sulfide, or FeS$_2$) is an important source of sulfur. This compound is sometimes called fool's gold because it looks so similar to gold.

volcanic deposits are the main source of sulfur. Today, vast underground deposits of relatively pure sulfur are found in association with salt domes located in the Louisiana swamplands of the United States and offshore in the Gulf of Mexico.

Sulfur from other sources

Sulfur can be extracted from several minerals. However, most of the world's sulfur occurs as a by-product of other industries. There are two main sources. One is sulfur that has to be removed from oil and natural gas during refining. The second is sulfur dioxide gas collected from metal-smelting plants and coal-burning power stations.

DID YOU KNOW?

THE FRASCH PROCESS

The Frasch process was developed by U.S. chemist Herman Frasch. It uses a system of pipes to recover sulfur from underground salt domes.

First a hole is drilled into the sulfur deposit, and a structure consisting of three pipes is driven down it. Superheated water is pumped down one pipe to melt the sulfur and compressed air goes down another to provide pressure. The molten sulfur, in the form of a foam, is forced to the surface through the third pipe and collected. Very pure sulfur is obtained this way.

Using the Frasch process, sulfur is pumped up from an underground deposit along the shore of the Mississippi River in Port Sulphur, Louisiana.

Chemistry and compounds

Sulfur is one of the most reactive of all the chemical elements. For example, it will burn readily in air to produce sulfur dioxide gas (SO_2). Some sulfur compounds are even more reactive than the element.

Chemistry of sulfur

Sulfur forms bonds with other atoms in two main ways. First, the sulfur atom may accept electrons from another atom, forming what is known as an ion (an electrically charged particle). In the compound sodium sulfide (Na_2S), for example, the sulfur atom accepts one electron from each sodium atom, becoming a sulfide ion (S^{2-}). The sulfide ion has eight rather than six electrons in its outermost electron shell, which is a more stable arrangement. Since each sodium atom loses one electron, each sodium ion is positively charged. As a result, the two elements are held together by electrical attraction. This kind of bond is called an electrovalent, or ionic, bond.

More usually, sulfur shares one or more of its electrons with another atom, forming a covalent bond. In hydrogen sulfide (H_2S), for example, the bond between the sulfur and each hydrogen atom consists of two shared electrons, one from each atom.

If a sample of sulfur powder is placed on a metal holder, ignited in air, and plunged into a gas jar filled with oxygen, the sulfur burns with a bright blue flame. The reaction produces sulfur dioxide gas.

Sulfur is a complex chemical element, however, because it can share several of its electrons in different circumstances. As a result, sulfur forms a variable number of bonds with other atoms. In most cases, however, the equivalent of four or six single bonds are formed.

Sulfur compounds

In industry, the most important compound of sulfur is sulfuric acid (H_2SO_4), which is described from pages 17 through 20. Due to its reactivity, sulfur reacts with many other elements, forming a vast range of compounds. Some of the more important sulfur compounds are described below.

Hydrogen sulfide

Hydrogen sulfide is a highly poisonous gas that burns in air with a blue flame to form sulfur dioxide. It is found in fossil fuels and is also produced by decaying matter. Since it is colorless, it can only be detected by its choking odor, similar to rotten eggs. Over time, however, hydrogen sulfide paralyzes nerves in the nose so that the smell appears to go away. This effect is potentially lethal, because the gas is so poisonous.

Sulfur dioxide

Sulfur dioxide is one of the most important sulfur gases. It is a dense, colorless, and poisonous gas with an unpleasant odor.

ATOMS AT WORK

Sulfur is an extremely reactive element. If sulfur is ignited in air and then introduced to a gas jar filled with oxygen, it burns with a bright blue flame.

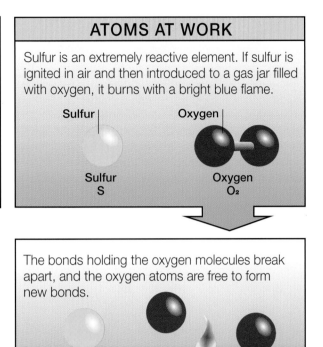

Sulfur
S

Oxygen
O_2

The bonds holding the oxygen molecules break apart, and the oxygen atoms are free to form new bonds.

Two oxygen atoms become attached to a sulfur atom, forming sulfur dioxide gas. Sulfur and all sulfur-containing compounds produce sulfur dioxide gas when they are burned in the presence of oxygen. Sulfur dioxide pollutes the atmosphere and is a major problem for the iron and copper refining industries, as well as for power stations burning sulfur-rich coal or oil.

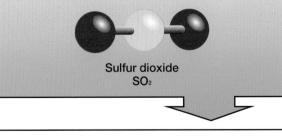

Sulfur dioxide
SO_2

The reaction that takes place when sulfur burns in oxygen can be written like this:

$$S + O_2 \rightarrow SO_2$$

This equation tells us that one atom of sulfur reacts with one molecule of oxygen to form one molecule of sulfur dioxide.

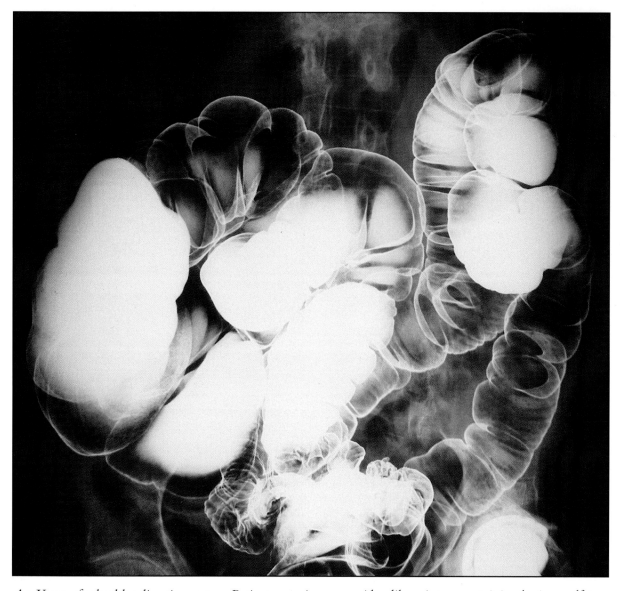

An X ray of a healthy digestive system. Patients are given a porridge-like mixture containing barium sulfate (BaSO₄), and the course of the "barium meal" through the digestive system is followed using X rays.

Sulfur dioxide is a by-product of many industrial processes. If it is released into the atmosphere, it mixes with water droplets to form acid rain. However it also has many valuable uses. For example, it is used to produce sulfuric acid and is a very good bleaching agent and food preservative.

Metal sulfides

Metal sulfides are simple compounds containing sulfur and one or more metals. Many are common minerals, and their major significance is as metal ores such as galena (lead sulfide, PbS) and chalcopyrite ($CuFeS_2$). Pyrite (iron sulfide, or FeS_2) is

GYPSUM

One of the most common sulfate minerals in Earth's crust is gypsum, which consists of two water molecules attached to a molecule of calcium sulfate. Its formula is $CaSO_4.2H_2O$. If gypsum is heated, most of the water is driven off, and the resulting product can be crushed into a fine powder called plaster of paris. If water is added to the powder, gypsum reforms and sets hard. This is how plaster works. The ornamental stone alabaster is also a form of gypsum.

the best known of the sulfides, mined for its sulfur content. Sodium sulfide (Na_2S) is used in the papermaking industry.

Sulfates and thiosulfates

Sulfates are compounds containing sulfur and oxygen in the form of the sulfate ion (SO_4^{2-}). Some, including copper sulfate ($CuSO_4$), are familiar high-school laboratory chemicals.

Sulfate salts tend to be stable and are often used as convenient ways of handling the metals they contain. For example, the poisonous metal barium, which is opaque to X rays, can be safely swallowed as insoluble barium sulfate ($BaSO_4$), to obtain X rays of the stomach and intestines.

Sodium sulfate (Na_2SO_4), or Glauber's salt, is commonly found in drinking water. It is used instead of sulfuric acid for some processes, for example, in the papermaking

and glassmaking industries. Magnesium sulfate or Epsom salts ($MgSO_4$) is used in medicine to encourage bowel movements.

When one of the four oxygen atoms in a sulfate ion is replaced by a second sulfur atom, the resulting ion is called a thiosulfate ion. An example is sodium

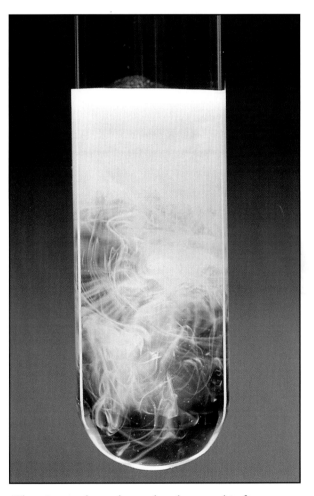

The picture above shows the photographic fixer reaction. The fixing agent, called sodium thiosulfate (the black substance at the bottom of the test tube), is dissolving silver bromide (AgBr, the cloudy solid suspended in solution). Silver bromide is used as the light-sensitive component of photographic film.

DAMAGING THE ENVIRONMENT

Sulfur gases are released naturally into the environment by volcanic activity and also by microorganisms. However, it is the industrial use of sulfur and its compounds that has resulted in many environmental problems. The main cause for concern is the release of sulfur dioxide into the atmosphere. This highly poisonous gas is one of the main pollutants responsible for acid rain.

When sulfur dioxide is released into the atmosphere, it dissolves in raindrops to produce a weak acid called sulfurous acid (H_2SO_3). However, sulfur dioxide also reacts with oxygen in the air to form sulfur trioxide (SO_3). When sulfur trioxide dissolves in water from the rain, it produces the stronger acid, sulfuric acid. Both acids damage vegetation, remove nutrients from soils, and increase the acidity of lakes and streams, harming the organisms that rely on the water supply. Sometimes, calcium oxide or lime (CaO) is added to lakes to reduce the acidity, but this is only a temporary solution.

Despite antipollution laws, acid rain remains a serious problem. For example, half of Canada's acid rain still comes from the United States. Some sources, such as copper smelters, are now fairly well controlled, but petrochemical plants remain serious polluters. They produce sulfur dioxide in low concentration but in enormous amounts. Collecting such vast amounts of the gas is an expensive process. The most cost-effective control method is to burn fewer fossil fuels.

thiosulfate or photographer's hypo ($Na_2S_2O_3$), which is used to "fix" photographs during processing.

Other sulfur compounds

Of the countless other sulfur compounds, sulfites (salts containing the SO_3^{2-} ion) are important in industry for bleaching. Carbon disulfide (CS_2) is an important industrial solvent. Sulfur also forms numerous other compounds with carbon.

The trees in the foreground of this picture have been damaged by acid rain, formed by the release of sulfur dioxide. The petrochemical plant in the background may be responsible for the release of this pollutant.

Sulfuric acid

Sulfuric acid is, perhaps, one of the most important inorganic chemicals. Worldwide, millions of tons of the acid are produced each year. Its uses in modern industry are countless.

Chemical properties

Pure sulfuric acid is a clear, dense, "oily" liquid, with a boiling point of 640°F (338°C). Its chemical formula is H_2SO_4.

Usually, concentrated sulfuric acid is diluted with water. When water and a concentrated acid are mixed, however, a large amount of heat is produced. If water is added to the acid, the water will immediately start to boil, causing it to splash out like hot oil in a frying pan. As a result, water should never be added to concentrated acid. Rather, the acid should be stirred slowly into the water.

Sulfuric acid is an extremely reactive compound. Dilute sulfuric acid will dissolve most metals, forming the metal sulfate and releasing hydrogen gas. Sulfuric acid will also react with basic (alkali) substances to produce a sulfate salt and water.

If a piece of magnesium is placed in a beaker of dilute sulfuric acid, magnesium sulfate ($MgSO_4$) is formed. Hydrogen gas is also released during the reaction.

Concentrated sulfuric acid is a dehydrating agent, which means it removes water from other compounds and mixtures. If concentrated acid is added to sugar, for example, all the water is removed from the sugar molecules, leaving a black lump of carbon. Since concentrated sulfuric acid is such a good dehydrating agent, it must never come into contact with the body. As soon as the acid touches human skin, the molecules in the skin immediately begin to lose water, forming an acid burn. For this reason, protective clothing and goggles should always be worn when dealing with concentrated sulfuric acid.

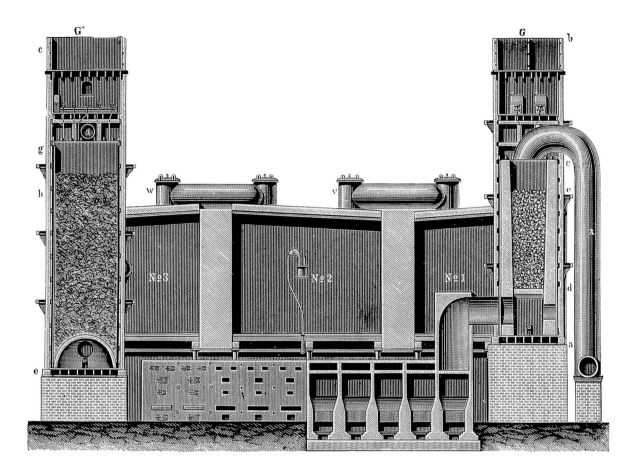

Manufacturing sulfuric acid

Sulfuric acid, once known by the name *oil of vitriol,* has been used for hundreds of years. The first industrial preparation of the acid, called the lead-chamber process, was developed in the 18th century. In this process, sulfuric acid was produced by oxidizing sulfur dioxide with moist air, using nitrogen oxide to catalyze (promote) the reaction. The reaction took place in large, boxlike chambers of sheet lead, from which the process got its name. Today, the lead-chamber process has largely been replaced by the contact process, invented in the 19th

This illustration shows a cross-section of the lead chambers used to produce sulfuric acid. The lead-chamber method of producing sulfuric acid was replaced by the contact process in the 20th century.

century. Contact-process plants produce sulfuric acid by reacting sulfur dioxide with oxygen and water (see page 20).

Using sulfuric acid

During the 19th century, the main use of sulfuric acid was in the manufacture of soda or sodium carbonate (Na_2CO_3), which was used in vast quantities to make

DID YOU KNOW?

AUTOMOBILE BATTERIES

Dilute sulfuric acid is used in automobile batteries. They are often called secondary batteries, because the cells (individual electrical circuits) inside the battery can be recharged. Each battery contains six cells, providing a total of 12 volts.

Most automobile batteries are of the lead-acid type. These work by converting chemical energy to electrical energy. Each of the cells inside the battery must have two electrodes, both made from a lead alloy. These electrodes must be immersed in a liquid called an electrolyte, which can conduct electricity as well as help the battery store electricity. Sulfuric acid is the electrolyte in lead-acid batteries.

soap and glass. By the end of the century, however, a new soda-making method had been developed that did not require the use of sulfuric acid.

Today, the amount of sulfuric acid in industry exceeds any other inorganic chemical. The biggest use for sulfuric acid is in the production of phosphate fertilizers. In the United States, for example, over 60 percent of the acid is used to convert phosphate rock ($Ca_3[PO_4]_2$) to phosphoric

Automobile batteries are stored in preparation for disposal. Since the batteries contain sulfuric acid, great care must be taken to insure their safe disposal.

acid (H_3PO_4), the starting chemical for the production of the extremely effective fertilizers known as superphosphates. The sulfur ends up as impure gypsum or calcium sulfate ($CaSO_4$), which is usually discarded as landfill, discharged into the sea, or used as plaster of paris.

Sulfuric acid is also used to make ammonium sulfate ($[NH_4]_2SO_4$), another important fertilizer. Other applications include the refining of petroleum, the removal of impurities from gasoline and kerosene, "pickling" steel (cleaning its surface), and the manufacture of other important chemicals, such as nitric and hydrochloric acids. Sulfuric acid is the electrolyte in lead-acid storage batteries, and it is also involved in the industrial preparation of artificial fibers, explosives, paints, paper, and textiles.

Other sulfur acids

There are many more sulfur acids, each having a different arrangement of the elements hydrogen, oxygen, and sulfur. For example, when sulfur dioxide is dissolved in water it produces another acid called sulfurous acid (H_2SO_3). However, sulfurous acid has never actually been isolated or detected. In fact, sulfurous acid is mainly dissolved sulfur dioxide, SO_2, of which a small proportion has reacted with water to form sulfite (SO_3^{2-}) ions and hydrogen sulfite (HSO^{3-}) ions.

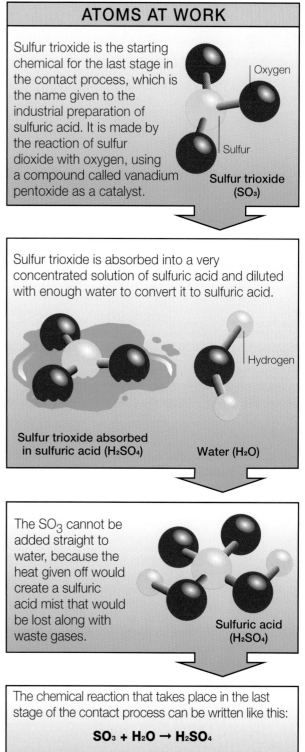

ATOMS AT WORK

Sulfur trioxide is the starting chemical for the last stage in the contact process, which is the name given to the industrial preparation of sulfuric acid. It is made by the reaction of sulfur dioxide with oxygen, using a compound called vanadium pentoxide as a catalyst.

Oxygen | Sulfur | Sulfur trioxide (SO_3)

Sulfur trioxide is absorbed into a very concentrated solution of sulfuric acid and diluted with enough water to convert it to sulfuric acid.

Sulfur trioxide absorbed in sulfuric acid (H_2SO_4) | Hydrogen | Water (H_2O)

The SO_3 cannot be added straight to water, because the heat given off would create a sulfuric acid mist that would be lost along with waste gases.

Sulfuric acid (H_2SO_4)

The chemical reaction that takes place in the last stage of the contact process can be written like this:

$$SO_3 + H_2O \rightarrow H_2SO_4$$

This shows us that one molecule of sulfur trioxide reacts with one molecule of water to produce one molecule of sulfuric acid.

From fossil fuels to rubber tires

This picture shows an oil refinery and adjoining sulfur plant in San Luis Obispo, California. Sulfur plants are often housed next to oil refineries, since fossil fuels contain high levels of sulfur.

Sulfur has an important place in the various large industries that process organic (carbon-containing) chemicals. Organic chemicals are the main constituents of fossil fuels, animal and plant tissues, and countless other derivative products. Since carbon is able to form molecules in the shape of long chains and rings, a huge variety of organic compounds exists.

Sometimes, sulfur is simply an unwanted element that needs to be removed during the processing of organic compounds.

Often, however, sulfur compounds play vital roles in the manufacturing of organic chemicals such as plastics or synthetic fibers. Numerous end products, such as dyes, for example, also contain sulfur.

Getting rid of sulfur

Coal, oil (petroleum), and natural gas usually contain sulfur compounds. Many of these compounds may be corrosive, poisonous, or pollute the environment. Some stop fuels from working efficiently; other simply smell bad.

*A striped skunk (*Mephitis mephitis*) adopts its distinctive defensive posture, ready to spray a foul-smelling, sulfur-containing liquid onto a predator.*

As a result, fossil fuels are "desulfurized" on a large scale. The process is also called "sweetening," especially when it involves getting rid of unpleasant odors. The first step in desulfurizing oil and natural gas is to react the sulfur-containing compounds with hydrogen, converting them to hydrogen sulfide gas. Sulfur is recovered from the hydrogen sulfide gas by reacting it with sulfur dioxide gas. Currently, efforts are being made to recover hydrogen from the hydrogen sulfide as well. The recovered hydrogen gas can then be reused as a fuel.

The desulfurization of coal is not so easy. Most of the sulfur in coal is burned to sulfur dioxide in power stations. Sulfur dioxide is a major pollutant, and it must not be released into the environment.

Sulfuric acid in oil refining

An important process in the oil refining industry is alkylation. In this process, the reaction of certain organic molecules causes chemical structures, such as double bonds between carbon atoms, to be removed. Harmful chemicals, such as benzene, are made harmless in this way. Sulfuric acid is the main chemical used to catalyze (promote) alkylation reactions. Indeed, millions of tons of sulfuric acid are used for this purpose every year. Sulfuric acid is also used in various other refining operations.

Detergents

Detergents are agents that remove grease and dirt. One end of the detergent molecule attracts water. The other end attracts fats and oils, removing them from the water. Most detergents include sulfur at the water-attracting end, usually in the form of a sulfonate group ($-SO^{3-}$). The sulfonate group is attached to a long chain of carbon atoms, which attracts the fats and oils. In the past, synthetic detergents polluted the environment because they were not biodegradable. Modern detergents are much more environmentally friendly.

Preservatives

Sulfur compounds, such as those containing the sulfite ion (SO_3^{2-}), are widely used to preserve food. Sulfur is poisonous to the

A man prepares a sulfur burner to protect his crop of apricots against spoilage by pests such as flies.

DISCOVERERS

CHARLES GOODYEAR

The process of vulcanizing rubber was discovered by U.S. inventor Charles Goodyear (1800–1860) in 1839. A trader in agricultural tools, Goodyear hit upon the process after treating rubber with various substances. He founded the Goodyear Rubber Company the following year to industrialize his process.

---

many pests, such as fungi and insects, that spoil food. Sulfur compounds work by removing oxygen from the air, preventing pests from getting the oxygen they need to breathe. Many sulfur compounds also create a mildly acidic environment in which organisms cannot survive.

Rubber

Natural rubber comes from the sap of the rubber tree (*Hevea brasiliensis*). It is an example of a polymer, which means it is made up of long chains of molecules.

Synthetic rubbers have also been made, each with different chemical compositions. Most are made from petrochemicals and vulcanized (heated with sulfur). Often, sulfur compounds are used to catalyze (promote) the reaction.

In some rubbers, sulfur atoms form part of the long-chain molecules themselves. These sulfur-based rubbers are particularly useful when the rubber has to be resistant to chemical attack.

ATOMS AT WORK

Rubber is a natural polymer made up of long chains of subunits, called monomers, containing the elements carbon and hydrogen. Rubber is a remarkable material. It can be stretched to at least twice its length and then return to its original length, over and over again. This is because the chains of carbon and hydrogen atoms can move relatively freely in relation to one another.

In a process called vulcanization, invented by Charles Goodyear, rubber is heated with sulfur. Sulfur atoms bond with the chains of rubber, and the resulting sulfur "bridges" hold the rubber chains together, making it harder for the rubber chains to move against one another. As a result, vulcanized rubber is much stronger than natural rubber. It does not soften as it is heated in the way that natural rubber does, so it can be used for tires and other applications where strength and resistance to wear are important.

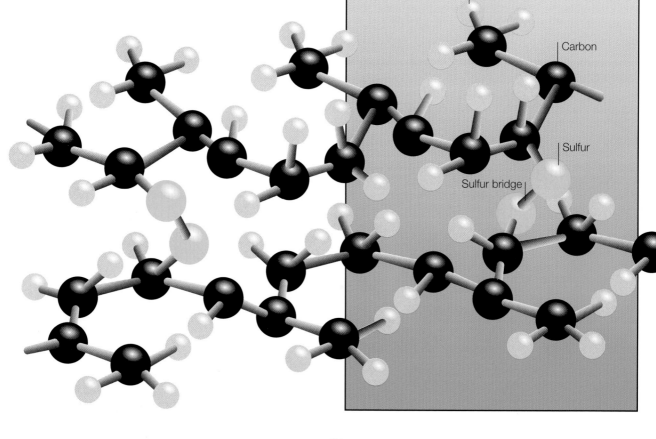

Hydrogen
Carbon
Sulfur
Sulfur bridge

Sulfur and warfare

Sulfur's most obvious contribution to warfare is its use in the manufacture of gunpowder and poisonous gas.

Gunpowder was the earliest explosive, invented by the Chinese about 1,000 years ago. When it came to Europe in the 1300s, it made possible the invention of firearms and totally changed the nature of warfare.

Gunpowder is a mixture of saltpeter (potassium nitrate, KNO_3), sulfur, and charcoal, all of which are ignited by a spark or flame. Today, the main modern use of gunpowder is in fireworks.

Another medieval invention, Greek fire, was a liquid that burned on contact with water. Its composition is unknown, but sulfur is likely to have been an ingredient.

This picture depicts the bombardment of Paris during the Franco-Prussian War (1870–1871). Gunpowder was replaced as a military explosive in 1900, when new "smokeless" powders were introduced.

Sulfur's later significance in explosives is indirect. Although sulfuric acid plays an important role in the manufacture of high explosives, high explosives themselves do not contain sulfur.

A sinister development in the 20th century was the manufacture and use of dichlorodiethyl sulfide—mustard gas—used intentionally to cause widespread injury and death. Mustard gas was first used in 1917, during World War I (1914–1918). When it is breathed into the lungs, it damages the cells on the lung lining. This causes fluid to leave the blood and fill the lungs, effectively drowning the victim. In small amounts, mustard gas forms blisters on the skin and causes permanent lung damage. A characteristic of mustard gas poisoning is that it causes blindness.

MUSTARD GAS

Mustard gas (dichlorodiethyl sulfide) is a highly poisonous substance that is made as an oily liquid. When it is released into the environment, it slowly evaporates as a gas.

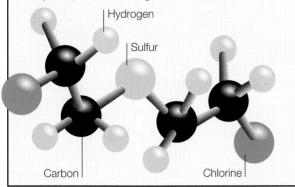

Hydrogen

Sulfur

Carbon

Chlorine

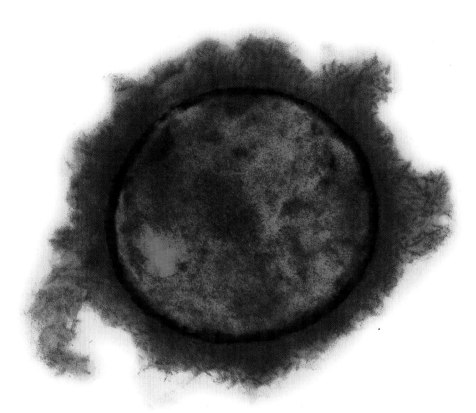

Biology and medicine

This picture shows an electron micrograph of a bacterium from the genus Desulphovibrio. *This bacterium is feeding on the sulfur from toxic waste.*

Animals, plants, and microorganisms would all die without sulfur. Sulfur-containing drugs can also play important roles in fighting disease.

Sulfur in biology

Green plants obtain sulfur in the form of sulfate ions. Taken up through the plant's roots, sulfur atoms are incorporated into many different organic (carbon-containing) compounds. Animals cannot process sulfate ions and rely on plants and bacteria to provide them with the sulfur they need.

Sulfur is an essential part of most proteins. Proteins are made from long chains of molecules called amino acids, some of which contain sulfur. Biological catalysts called enzymes are proteins. They regulate biochemical reactions within the body. In an enzyme, the chains of amino acids fold up into ball-like shapes. The structure of the enzyme has to be exactly right for it to work properly. Sulfur-containing amino acids play a role in this. By forming cross-links, called disulfide

DID YOU KNOW?

BACTERIA AND SULFUR

Bacteria are a vital part of the sulfur cycle—the transfer of sulfur between different parts of the living and nonliving environment.

Some bacteria can obtain energy directly from sulfur compounds, such as hydrogen sulfide and iron sulfide. Others use them in place of oxygen or to help with photosynthesis (producing food using light energy from the Sun).

At some hydrothermal vents—volcanic formations on the seafloor—bacteria live a unique lifestyle inside giant tube worms. Hydrogen sulfide rising from Earth's crust is trapped by the worms' red hemoglobin pigment and is then processed by the bacteria. They use the energy they gain to make organic (carbon-containing) compounds, which the worms absorb as food.

bridges, with each other, the sulfur-containing amino acids help the enzymes to keep their structures rigid.

Sulfur is also needed for smaller, but equally vital, biological molecules, such as biotin—one of the B group vitamins.

Medicine and health

Sulfur compounds have been used in the treatment of many illnesses since ancient times. The ancient Egyptians, for example, used sulfur as a traditional remedy for various ailments. More recently in the 1930s, drugs containing sulfur, called sulfonamides or sulfa drugs, were developed to combat disease. These were the first effective drugs for combating many bacterial infections. Sulfa drugs work by destroying the enzyme that is needed for the growth of bacterial cells. Sulfa drugs were partly replaced by antibiotics such as penicillin, but they still remain useful forms of treatment today.

Many sulfur compounds can also promote health through their use as bleaches, disinfectants, and preservatives.

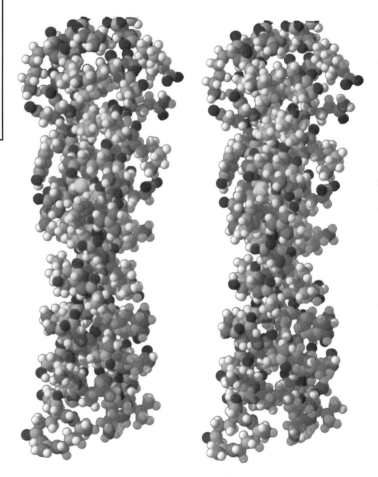

This image shows two molecules of the protein keratin, found in skin, hair, and nails. Sulfur atoms (yellow) enable the molecules to extend and contract.

Periodic table

Everything in the universe is made from combinations of substances called elements. Elements are the building blocks of matter. They are made of tiny atoms, which are much too small to see.

The character of an atom depends on how many even tinier particles called protons there are in its center, or nucleus. An element's atomic number is the same as the number of protons.

Scientists have found around 110 different elements. About 90 elements occur naturally on Earth. The rest have been made in experiments.

All these elements are set out on a chart called the periodic table. This lists all the elements in order according to their atomic number.

The elements at the left of the table are metals. Those at the right are nonmetals. Between the metals and the nonmetals are the metalloids, which sometimes act like metals and sometimes like nonmetals.

● On the left of the table are the alkali metals. These elements have just one electron in their outer shells.

● On the right of the periodic table are the noble gases. These elements have full outer shells.

● Elements in the same group have the same number of electrons in their outer shells.

● Elements get more reactive as you go down a group.

● The number of electrons orbiting the nucleus increases down each group.

● The transition metals are in the middle of the table, between Groups II and III.

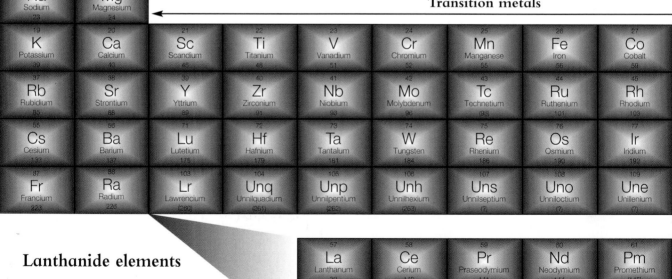

The horizontal rows are called periods. As you go across a period, the atomic number increases by one from each element to the next. The vertical columns are called groups. Elements get heavier as you go down a group. All the elements in a group have the same number of electrons in their outer shells. This means they react in similar ways.

The transition metals fall between Groups II and III. Their electron shells fill up in an unusual way. The lanthanide elements and the actinide elements are set apart from the main table to make it easier to read. All the lanthanide elements and the actinide elements are quite rare.

Sulfur in the table

Sulfur is found on the right-hand side of the periodic table among the nonmetals. It has an atomic number of 16, which tells us there are 16 protons and 16 electrons inside each atom. Sulfur reacts with metals and nonmetals to form a huge number of different compounds. Many of these are extremely useful to humans.

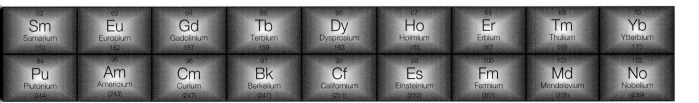

Chemical reactions

Chemical reactions are going on all the time—candles burn, nails rust, food is digested. Some reactions involve just two substances; others many more. But whenever a reaction takes place, at least one substance is changed.

In a chemical reaction, the atoms stay the same. But they join up in different combinations to form new molecules.

Writing an equation

Chemical reactions can be described by writing down the atoms and molecules before and the atoms and molecules after. Since the atoms stay the same, the number of atoms before will be the same as the number of atoms after; only the molecules change. Chemists write the reaction as a chemical equation.

When the numbers of each atom on both sides of the equation are equal, the equation is balanced.

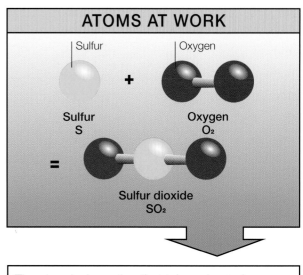

ATOMS AT WORK

Sulfur

Oxygen

+

Sulfur
S

Oxygen
O_2

=

Sulfur dioxide
SO_2

The chemical reaction that takes place when sulfur burns in oxygen looks like this:

$$S + O_2 \rightarrow SO_2$$

The number of sulfur atoms and oxygen atoms is the same on both sides of the equation.

If the numbers are not equal, something must be wrong. So the chemist looks at the equation again and adjusts the number of atoms involved until the equation balances.

A pile of sulfur waits for shipment at the Port of Vancouver in Canada.

Glossary

acid rain: When certain gases rise into the atmosphere, they dissolve in rainwater, making the rain acidic.

allotrope: A different form of the same element in which the atoms are arranged in a different pattern.

atom: The smallest part of an element that has all the properties of that element.

atomic number: The number of protons in an atom.

bond: The attraction between two atoms that holds them together.

catalyst: Something that makes a reaction occur more quickly.

compound: A substance that is made of atoms of more than one element.

electron: A tiny particle with a negative charge. Electrons are found inside atoms, where they move around the nucleus in layers called electron shells.

fossil fuel: A fuel, such as coal, oil, or natural gas, that is formed in the earth from plant and animal remains.

fungicide: A substance that destroys fungi or prevents their growth.

inorganic chemical industry: The industry that manufactures all chemicals that are not predominantly carbon-based.

ion: A particle of an element similar to an atom but carrying an additional negative or positive electrical charge.

isotopes: Atoms of an element with the same number of protons and electrons but different numbers of neutrons.

mineral: Chemical elements joined together as compounds, usually obtained from the ground.

neutron: A tiny particle with no electrical charge. It is found in the nucleus of every atom.

nonmetal: An element on the right-hand side of the periodic table.

nucleus: The center of an atom. It contains protons and neutrons.

ore: A collection of minerals from which metals, in particular, are usually extracted.

oxidation: A reaction where oxygen is added, or one or more electrons are removed, from a substance.

periodic table: A chart of all the chemical elements laid out in order of their atomic number.

products: The substances formed in a chemical reaction.

proton: A tiny particle with a positive charge. Protons are found inside the nucleus of an atom.

reactants: The substances that react together in a chemical reaction.

refining: An industrial process that frees substances, such as fossil fuels, from impurities or unwanted material.

vulcanization: A process whereby rubber is heated with sulfur to make the rubber stronger and more resistant to wear.

Index